GIRLS WILL BE GIRLS

GIRLS WILL BE GIRLS

A PLAY

Francis Jarman

THE BORGO PRESS
An Imprint of Wildside Press
Rockville, Maryland

MMVII

First published in Germany in 2000
by LIBRI Books on Demand GmbH, Norderstedt

Cover graphics by Titus Twister

THIS EDITION FIRST PUBLISHED IN 2007

FROM THE PREFACE TO THE 2000 EDITION

'Any resemblance to persons living or dead is purely coincidental' (or words to that effect).

That's what it often says, usually in very small print, on the imprint page at the beginning of a published work of fiction. Is it ever really true, though? If you stop to think about it, how can you invent fictional characters without any reference (however trivial) to people that you've known? Each of your characters will always be a mosaic of qualities and quirks remembered from people in real life, perhaps with a certain element of wild personal fantasy thrown in as well. But the mosaic is never identical with a real person. However much the light shining off individual pieces may remind you for a moment of John, or Bill, or Mary, the fictional character will always be a composite, and if it isn't, you aren't writing fiction. In the present case no real person need take offence (and certainly no-one in the music industry, of which I have no personal knowledge worth mentioning). Let me put it on record that there has been no Lisa, Rickie, Sally or Sammie (or any of the other characters) in my life, although I hope that the pieces of each mosaic fit together well enough to make you believe that there could have been such a person.

As for that 'element of wild personal fantasy' – most writers allow themselves one heroine per story, or two at the most, but I've given myself a whole pop group to play with, plus a couple of other women characters with quite a lot going for them! There is a dangerous dilemma here, because as an author you're between Scylla and Charybdis, the devil and the deep blue sea. If there really is (you claim) no 'resemblance to persons living or dead' in your fiction, does that mean that what you are offering people is a street map of your subconscious? After seeing a performance of my first play, *A Star Fell*, which is about massacre and rape among other things, someone wrote to me to express admiration for my courage in *revealing my personal experiences and thoughts in public* in such a way. Whoa! I thought, let's not jump to hasty conclusions about this particular author's repressed fantasies. (Incidentally, *Girl Will Be Girls* has no rapes or massacres, though at one point somebody does get punched on the nose.)

If I didn't then know the girls personally, as real people, could it be that the idea for the girl pop group came from the media? Are the four girls intended to represent a famous group like ----------, or perhaps even The ----------? No, of course they aren't. Or am I trying, more indirectly, to make some profound critical statement about people in groups like these? No, I'm not. Admittedly, I do make fun of the girls a little (which is my good right, since I invented them), but I hope that I do it in an affectionate way... The girls as you see them on stage are simply there to amuse you, and to entertain you with their music (which is what I've imagined it is that they do to earn a living). There is absolutely nothing to be gained from assuming that they're based on people who earn their living in such a way in real life.

Finally, there's the problem of when the play takes place... The songs, written and arranged by my friends Paul Harrison, Matthias Müller and Paul Willin,[1] have got a strong touch of the Sixties, whereas the language used by the characters seems to hint at a date around 1970. You may notice the odd thing that 'wasn't around in those days' or that 'people didn't say like that'... Still, I'm not going to lose any sleep worrying about the anachronisms, because *Girls Will Be Girls* is not an exercise in popular ethnography, it's just a bit of fun that I hope you'll enjoy watching or reading (as I enjoyed writing it). The play does have a message, though – but I'll leave it to *you* to find it.

- Francis Jarman

---

[1] The soundtrack of *Girls Will Be Girls* is available on CD (Rays LC 05979). For further information, please write to: Matthias Müller, c/o IfAS, University of Hildesheim, Marienburger Platz 22, 31141 Hildesheim, Germany.

INTRODUCTION (2007)

I should have added a couple of lines to the Preface
that I wrote in 2000, saying something about the
pretty peculiar way in which *Girls Will Be Girls* came
to written. I first had the idea for the play while
walking along the beach in Corfu, Greece, in the
spring of 1998. It was a cold, wet, windy day, and the
beach was grubby. However, I wasn't in Corfu for a
holiday, but on a teaching assignment at the Ionian
University. In my free time I did some sightseeing,
and between classes I went for walks, and it was on
one of these walks that I suddenly found myself
thinking that my second play, after the rather earnest
A Star Fell, ought to be a comedy, and why not a
comedy about a pop group? Moreover: To maximise
the possibilities for humorous romantic misunder-
standings, why not make the group a girl band?

Back in Germany again (I've spent most of my adult
life there, working as a university teacher), I drafted a
first version of the play over a long weekend, using
plastic figures from my daughter's Lego building set
to help with the complexities of the plot. At least one
or two songs were needed to give the band some
credibility, and these would be provided by my
colleague Paul Harrison, who is a gifted songwriter.
In the spring of 1999, Paul and I were both in
Portugal, teaching in universities at different ends of
the country. We arranged to meet – he travelled down
to Lisbon for a weekend, and a week later I took the

train up to Oporto. We sat in cafés to talk, or talked as we wandered around looking at the sights. I read him scenes from the play, he sang me the songs, and (though I can't imagine what the local people thought the two mad Englishmen were up to) it proved to be a very creative couple of days. Lisbon even contributed a detail to the text – Ronnie's erotic musings about Sammie ('The way she runs her hand through her hair...') were based on a little scene that I observed one afternoon in the park at the Museu Calouste Gulbenkian.

The number of songs increased rapidly, and more song material was contributed by Paul Willin, who would be directing the first production of the play. The whole musical side of the project was put in the hands of Matthias Müller, who arranged the songs, coached the singers, and organised the backing musicians. Katrin Ebert trained an enthusiastic troupe of go-go dancers. *Girls Will Be Girls* was a genuine team-effort, and a huge success, attracting media attention and featuring in several programmes on local television (quite an achievement for a foreign-language show!). By popular demand, the production was revived six months later as a 'Christmas Special'.

Since then, the play has been translated into German[2] and staged in Berlin (2005) under the direction of

---

[2] Francis Jarman, *Girls Will Be Girls – Mädchen eben!* Translated by Paul Harrison. Norderstedt: Books on Demand, 2005, ISBN 3-8334-3564-X.

Christine Barker. In addition to producing the translation, Paul Harrison reprised in Berlin the role (Ronnie) that he had created in the original Hildesheim production, while Burkhard Schäfer, the original Allan, 'guested' in Berlin as Gus, the rock journalist.

A few small changes have been made to the text for this new international edition.

– Francis Jarman

CHARACTERS

- The Girls:

Sally *('the young one')*
Sammie *('the funny one')*
Lisa *('the sensitive one')*
Rickie *('the clever one')*

- Their management:

Elaine, *their tour manager*
Steve, *the equipment manager*
Ronnie de Silver (Jonquil), *their agent*

- Friends and visitors:

Linda, *a fan*
Sharon, *another fan*
Vero (Veronica), *Lisa's girlfriend*
Gus, *from the* New Musical Chronicle
Allan, *the photographer*

The scene of the play is Elaine's large house in an expensive part of London.

Girls Will Be Girls was first presented in the Auditorium Maximum of Hildesheim University on June 5th, 2000 by the English Drama Group of the University with the following cast:

Sally	**Valerie Baucke**
Sammie	**Judy Bersem**
Lisa	**Sandra Bettels**
Rickie	**Christina Richter**
Elaine	**Carolin Werthmüller**
Steve	**Jörg Petzold**
Ronnie de Silver (Jonquil)	**Paul Harrison**
Linda	**Isabelle Peters**
Sharon	**Ulrike Michiels**
Vero (Veronica)	**Silvia Grimmsmann**
Gus	**Olaf Schulz**
Allan	**Burkhard Schaefer**

The dancers
Ingvild Bode, **Anika Dethlefsen**, **Katrin Ebert**, **Aditya Eggert**, **Mathilde Gervais**, **Ulrike Michiels**, **Elena Navarro**, **Isabelle Peters**

The musicians
Matti Mueller (keyboards), **Jan Christian Baumgartner** (guitar), **Felix Blohmer** (tenor sax), **Christian Lubrich** (bass), **Michael Deiters** (drums)

The songs were written by **Paul Harrison** and **Paul Willin**

Song arrangements and musical direction by **Matthias Müller**

Choreography by **Katrin Ebert**

Prompt: **Susanne Schrader**

Directed by **Paul Willin**

PART ONE

[1]

Prologue: In front of ELAINE's *house.* LISA *and* VERO *are looking at each other very intently. They embrace and kiss. There is the sudden light of a camera-flash. They look round in surprise. Then darkness.*

[2]

Screams and shouts from FANS *in different parts of the auditorium.*

FANS *[different voices].* Aaargh! It's The Girls! Lisa! Rickie! Sammy! Sally! Let me touch you! We love you, Lisa! Aaargh! etc.

[SONG 1: Only a Kiss]

It is now some hours after the incident in front of the house. The lights come up to reveal SALLY, STEVE *and* ELAINE.

SALLY. Well, it was only a kiss.

STEVE. Yeah.

ELAINE *[looking heavenwards].* God give me patience!

STEVE. What's wrong with a kiss? Boys kiss girls. I kiss Rickie all the time, don't I?

SALLY. That's right. Girls kiss boys. I kiss... *[With false coyness]* Well, I'm sure you all know!

STEVE. You bet! *[To* ELAINE*]* And Sally kisses her grandma, too.

SALLY. Steve kisses Pedro – the gay bloke from the wine-bar.

STEVE *[embarrassed]*. No I don't! Well, not like *that*.

ELAINE *[exasperated]*. Have you two quite finished?

STEVE *[shrugging]*. So what's wrong with a kiss?

ELAINE *[still exasperated]*. Women-do-not-kiss-other-women. That's what.

SALLY. Oh, come on! In the band we're always kissing each other. Even in front of the fans. Like at concerts.

ELAINE *[still exasperated]*. Sally, where were you when the big chief in the sky handed out those little pills with 'I.Q.' written on them?

SALLY. What do you mean?

ELAINE. I'm sure that you and Rickie and Sammie

and Lisa peck at each other like battery hens on a hot afternoon.

SALLY. So?

ELAINE. Well, since when has this sisterly affection meant that you wanted to hump each other? *[Pause]* Lisa and Vero were almost *eating each other*, for chrissake! And somebody had to go and take a photograph!

STEVE. Now be reasonable, Elaine. What do you expect them to do? They're in love. I mean, personally I don't see the point of this lesbian business –

ELAINE. Now that's hardly surprising.

STEVE. – a bit of a waste, if you ask me. But it is their right, isn't it?

ELAINE. That picture will be in every newspaper that our fans read. Oh, it won't be in the *Guardian*, the *Observer* or the *Times*, I grant you that. But it *will* be on the front page of the *Daily Tit* and the *Sunday Filth*. And think of the headlines! 'Lezzie Lesson in Love for Lovely Lisa.' 'Girl Group Singer Goes For Girls.' 'Lisa Loves a Lady.' And the *name* of the group won't help either. 'The Girls.' Think what they'll make of that! *[Gloomily]* Then we're finished.

SALLY. I still don't see it.

ELAINE. Sally, sweetheart, remember when we were thinking up labels for the people in the band?

STEVE. Oh I can remember that. 'Rickie the clever one.' 'Lisa the sensitive one.' Umm... 'Sammie the funny one.' And 'Sally –'

ELAINE *[to* SALLY, *brutally]*. We originally had you pencilled in as 'the thick one', but it wasn't a good marketing concept.

SALLY. Well, thank you!

STEVE *[too late]*. – 'Sally the young one!'

ELAINE. Let me spell it out for you, dear. I have nothing against Vero. I'm sure she's a delightful individual. O.K.?

STEVE. I think we all agree on that.

ELAINE. Thank you, Steve. Having said that, there is *no way* that our spotty adolescent fans are going to accept that one of their idols is a raging queer who sleeps with women! Do you get me? We're not talking about intellectuals. We're not talking about students. We're not even talking about normal adults. We're talking about confused teenage girls for whom our Lisa is... an older sister! An *identification figure*! *[Again, emphatically]* Do I make myself clear? We have a crisis.

STEVE. And where *is* the identification figure?

ELAINE. Upstairs, asleep.

STEVE. I'll go and fetch her. *[He sets off]* Hey, who are you? *[He returns, pulling* LINDA *with him]*

LINDA *[indignant]*. Don't pull me arm off! *[Seeing* SALLY*]* Oh! You're Sally, aren't you? Can I touch you? I've never touched one of The Girls before! *[Now* STEVE *has to hold her back]*

STEVE. That's the second one today! Must be at least a dozen this week!

SALLY. Ugh! Keep her off me!

ELAINE. O.K., Sally don't overreact. These *are* our fans, you know!

LINDA. That was me on Tuesday, too. *[To* STEVE*]* Hey, lay off!

ELAINE. Look, love, we're having a busy day. We love our fans – don't we Sally?

SALLY *[unenthusiastically]*. Sure.

ELAINE. But you are, if I might say so, *in the way*.

LINDA. Can't I stay a bit? Sort of... *watch*, like?

ELAINE [*firmly*]. No, love. [STEVE *bundles her out*]
Bye bye! Oh dear oh dear! We need everyone here.
We need a strategy.

STEVE [*returning*]. We were going to meet anyway to
run through the new material. I'll ring Rickie.

ELAINE. I already have. And I told her to stop on the
way and get some takeaway food for everyone.

SALLY. Good, I'm starving!

ELAINE. Sammie's already on her way over. They
both know.

STEVE. So the whole gang will be here?

ELAINE. No, there's someone else we need. *[Pause]*
Ronnie!

SALLY [*appalled*]. Oh no! Not Ronnie! He thinks he's
God's gift! He's *creepy*. Why do we need *him*?

ELAINE. Because, sweetheart, he organises our
earnings. I'm only your tour manager, remember?
Who books the tours? Who arranges the concerts?
Who sets up our recording contracts? Who is Mr.
Money?

SALLY. O.K., O.K.

ELAINE [*to* SALLY]. Sally, *you* go and get Lisa. Wake

her *gently*, though. *[SALLY exits]*

STEVE *[with mild irony]*. She will go far, that girl.

ELAINE. I wish she would. Some remote island in the middle of the Pacific might be a good start.

STEVE. She doesn't like Ronnie very much, does she?

ELAINE. Once upon a time... he had his evil way with her.

STEVE. She must have been very drunk!

ELAINE. No, it wasn't like that. But he lost interest – a bit too quickly.

STEVE. Oh.

ELAINE. And we girls don't take kindly to that.

STEVE. No, I'm sure you don't.

ELAINE. Let's see if he's there. *[ELAINE rings RONNIE]* Hello. It's Elaine. *[Pause]* And the same to you with bells on it. Look, Ronnie, we need you here *now. [Pause]* How do you know? Who told you? *[Pause]* Rickie? That girl is too clever for her own good. *[Pause]* O.K., as soon as you can. *[Pause]* Oh, charming! You haven't lost your touch, have you? *[Laughs]* You dirty beast! O.K., till then. *[Catching STEVE's eye as she puts down the phone]* Yes, he had his evil way with me, too. But it's a long time ago. *[Pause]* And I got over it, didn't I?

[3]

Enter SAMMIE.

SAMMIE. Hello, everyone. Just you two here?

ELAINE. No, Lisa's sleeping upstairs. Sally's gone to wake her.

SAMMIE. Sleeping? Bit early for that, isn't it? Bit decadent? Is this Lady Lesbia's new lifestyle?

ELAINE. Cut it out, Sammie. We've got enough difficulties as it is.

SAMMIE. Well, that's no fault of *mine*, is it?

ELAINE. Try and be *constructive. [Enter* SALLY*]*

SALLY. She'll be down in a sec. *[Seeing* SAMMIE*, and without enthusiasm]* Oh, hello.

SAMMIE. How's the youth department, then? Got the pimple crisis sorted out yet?

SALLY. Bugger off.

ELAINE. Look, I'm getting rather fed up with this.

And it's not fair on Steve.

STEVE [*surprised*]. Oh, I'll survive.

SALLY. Well she shouldn't keep on getting at me, should she?

SAMMIE. There's something about you that just asks for it. [ELAINE *gives her a black look*] Alright, alright.

STEVE. When's Rickie coming?

ELAINE. She should be here any moment now. [*Enter* LISA]

STEVE [*turning*]. Oh, Rickie!... [*Then disappointed*] Oh, it's you.

LISA [*still tired*]. Sorry to disappoint you, Steve.

SAMMIE [*to* LISA]. Just look what you've got us into! Couldn't you keep your hands off her? I ask you! On the front-doorstep!

LISA [*tired*]. Yes, yes.

SAMMIE. And right in front of the gentlemen of the Press!

ELAINE. It was only *one* photographer, wasn't it, Lisa?

SAMMIE. A week from now that bloody photograph will be syndicated all round the world.

ELAINE. Well, that means we've still got time, doesn't it? A couple of days at least. Whoever took that photo, they'll be greedy, won't they? They'll be trying to sell it now. Looking for the highest bidder. We need to find a way of stopping it.

STEVE [hearing a sound]. Wasn't that the door? That'll be Rickie.

SAMMIE. And about time too.

RICKIE enters carrying bags with takeaway Chinese food, paper plates, plastic cutlery, etc. STEVE greets her with rather naïve enthusiasm.

STEVE. Hello, darling!

RICKIE [as STEVE embraces her clumsily]. Hey, mind the food! Talk about sex-starved!

SALLY [doing a mocking imitation]. Oooh, darling!

RICKIE [laughing]. It started with a kiss...

ELAINE [irritated]. Yes, and it was all this kissing around that got us into trouble in the first place!

SAMMIE. Well, they don't do it on the doorstep, do they?

24

LISA [turning away]. Thank you.

SAMMIE [to LISA, unpleasantly]. Got the sulks?

LISA. I'm not in the mood.

SAMMIE. Suit yourself.

RICKIE [with a dramatic gesture]. Mesdames et messieurs, dinner is served!

They settle themselves on the floor around the food, LISA last and obviously unwillingly. STEVE remains standing.

STEVE. I'm not hungry. Hey, I'll leave you girls to it. Just make sure you get it together before eight o'clock, O.K.? None of this squabbling, please. [To RICKIE] I'll go round to Lennie's for a beer. I'll see you later, sweetheart. [STEVE moves off, then returns again dragging LINDA, a fan] Not you again! This is no bloody joke!

LINDA [wailing]. But I love them! Aaargh! They're all there! Lisa! It is Lisa! Sammie! [Reaching out her free hand] We love you! Please! Let me stay!

RICKIE. Oh, help!

Another fan, SHARON, almost manages to slip past, but STEVE catches her with his other hand.

STEVE. No you don't!

SHARON *[hysterical, holding out her autograph album]*. Lisa! Write 'I love you, Sharon'. *Please!!*

LINDA *[wailing, holding out hers]*. No, write Linda! *Linda!* Oh, I'm going to be sick!

SALLY. Oh no!

STEVE *[to* LINDA, *as he drags the fans away]*. Why is it always *girls* who break in? If you were a *bloke*, I bet nobody would even notice you. You shouldn't be wasting your time like this! Anyway, don't take it personal. I'm only trying to give you some good advice.

LINDA. Thanks, grandpa, you already have!

SHARON *[to* LINDA*]*. What do you mean?

LINDA *[to* SHARON*]*. Wait and see!

STEVE. Anyway, why can't you have a crush on some goodlooking *fella*, somebody like me, for example?

LINDA *[to* SHARON*]*. What do you reckon? Did they make him stupid or did he learn it all by himself?

STEVE *[now very annoyed]*. Out! Out! *[Exeunt* STEVE, LINDA *and* SHARON*]*

[SONG 2: I've Got a Crush on You]

[4]

SAMMIE. So it's just *mesdames*, then! *[To* RICKIE, *unenthusiastically]* *Where* did you say you bought this?

RICKIE. Andy's Diner. They do Chinese stuff as well. Yeah, I know, it's not fantastic. Steve likes going there with the band after a show. It's cheap. The service is quick. And they don't mind if you, er *[Mimicking vividly]* throw up in the bar. Well, not if you're a regular customer they don't mind. Not that I ever *do* throw up in the bar, of course!

SAMMIE *[picking out and holding up a bit of meat of dubious appearance].* Yes, but what's this? What was it when it was still alive? *[Pause]* And how long has it been dead?

RICKIE *[irritated].* Don't start getting picky with *me*. You've eaten worse things than that. Just think of that tour in the northeast. Gateshead...

ELAINE. Oh, god, yes.

SAMMIE. Is it *meat*?

RICKIE. Now *there's* an interesting question.

SALLY. I went there a couple of weeks ago.

SAMMIE. What, Gateshead?

SALLY. No, you know, Andy's Diner. With Gus from the *Chronicle*.

SAMMIE. Not *the* Gus?

RICKIE. From *the* one and only *New Musical Chronicle*?

SAMMIE. I don't believe a word of it.

SALLY. He invited me out.

RICKIE. What a cavalier!

SAMMIE. And what a romantic rendezvous!

SALLY *[not noticing how they are winding her up]*. He paid for everything. And for the taxi afterwards.

RICKIE *[sings]*. 'Hey, big spender!'

SAMMIE. He paid for *everything*?

RICKIE. I didn't know you were that sort of girl!

SALLY. He's a very deeply sensitive person.

RICKIE *[winking to* SAMMIE*]*. Oh, I bet he is!

SAMMIE. And what love-nest did the taxi take you to... *afterwards*?

SALLY *[burbling happily on]*. Actually, he says Andy's is his regular watering-hole. All the *Chronicle* people go there. That's what he calls it – his watering-hole.

RICKIE. What a disgusting expression. Almost urological.

SAMMIE. But it does explain the way he writes. *[Resigned]* Well, you are what you eat, they say. And what you drink.

SALLY. Gus says that, at places like Andy's, if you're sober enough to ask questions about what's in the food, you're not drunk enough to want to eat it when it arrives.

SAMMIE. What a witty fellow! I shall remember him in about an hour's time.

SALLY. Why?

SAMMIE. Because by then I shall probably be vomiting my supper into the toilet bowl.

RICKIE. Well, *I'm* hungry. *[Lifting one of the container lids]* I don't know what you lot are complaining about. It looks smashing. And it smells...*[She realises that it doesn't actually smell* *very good]* er... well, O.K. I suppose.

They eat, RICKIE, SALLY *and* SAMMIE *greedily.* LISA *shows little interest.*

ELAINE *[offering* LISA *something].* Here, Lisa, have some of this.

LISA. No, it's alright.

SALLY *[grabbing at it].* Well I won't say no.

RICKIE *[to* SAMMIE*].* Pass the sauce over?

SAMMIE. Then give us some rice.

SALLY *[to* RICKIE*].* I'll finish the sauce.

RICKIE *[to* SALLY*].* Hands off!

SAMMIE *[to* SALLY*].* You've already had your share.

SALLY. No I haven't.

SAMMIE. You greedy cow!

ELAINE. Lisa hasn't had *any* yet.

SALLY. That's her bad luck.

ELAINE *[taking the sauce].* No, let Lisa have the rest!

SALLY *[indignantly].* I can't eat all this without any sauce! I'm not Chinese, you know!

RICKIE *[making slit-eyes].* Ha, so!

SAMMIE. Confucius he say...

RICKIE. Velly good lice!

SALLY. Oh, shut up!

RICKIE. Big girls don't cly.

SALLY *[furious].* You both think you're so smart, don't you? 'The clever one.' 'The funny one.' Ha ha ha. I'll tell Gus what you're *really* like and he'll put it in the *Chronicle* and *then* we'll see who's laughing!

RICKIE *[putting down her paper plate].* Hey! That's it! That is *it*!

They all look at her.

ELAINE. Eh?

SALLY. Yer wot?

SAMMIE. I think Rickie's having kittens.

RICKIE. No, listen. Listen carefully. As I see it, there are three things we can do about that bloody photo. The first is: just ride it out. Let them do their worst.

Kids these days know what lesbians are, surely? O.K., we'd lose some of them. Some of the parents would freak out, I suppose. And I don't think the recording company would be very happy...

ELAINE. We've got too many competitors, Rickie, just waiting to step in. And they're all as pure as the driven snow.

SAMMIE. Oh, come on! You must be joking! I could tell you a thing or two...

ELAINE. No, in public they're clean. Just like us... until now.

LISA *[bitter]*. So I'm dirty, am I?

ELAINE *[to* LISA, *gently]*. No, darling, of course not. But you know what I mean, don't you? *[To the whole group]* Look, you're an image band. It's the image they buy, not the music. You want to throw the image away? I'm sorry, I'm not prepared to take the risk. There's too much money riding on this.

LISA *[quietly]*. I could leave the group. That would solve the problem, wouldn't it?

ELAINE *[to* LISA, *firmly]*. Stop it, Lisa, there's no need for that.

RICKIE. Alright, that's settled then. The second thing is: we could just deny it. O.K.? Say it's a fake. That they staged it. They manipulated it. Magazines do it all the time.

ELAINE. I don't think that'd work.

RICKIE. No, nor do I. And the third thing is...

SAMMIE. Er... suicide?

ELAINE. Someone goes round to buy back the photo?

RICKIE. We might not have enough money for that.

SAMMIE. One of us offers herself to the photographer?

SALLY. Shouldn't *Lisa* do that? She caused all this.

LISA. Don't be so cheap.

RICKIE. Actually, we *do* need something like that. *[Giving* SALLY *a cunning look]* But if anyone's going to be putting their charms on offer, it'll have to be... you, Sally!

SALLY *[outraged]*. What?!! How come?

RICKIE. Don't freak out, Sally. You have a key role to play, but we'll come to that in a moment. *[Turning to the others]* Listen, I'll explain. Our third possibility, right? We can kill this story, and do you know how? We can kill it by making it seem worthless!

ELAINE. How?

RICKIE. Nobody'll believe it was just a goodbye kiss at the front door, will they? But if we put out a story, very quickly, about Lisa and her *new boyfriend.* You know – photos, interviews, background, the whole caboodle.

LISA. This is perverse! What are you talking about? Who is this 'boyfriend'?

RICKIE. It has to be someone we can trust. Someone who's been seen around with Lisa. Someone who won't try to take advantage of the situation. Someone we've known a long time. Someone in the family. Someone dependable. Reliable. Good. Solid. Unimaginative. Do we *know* anyone like that?

STEVE *wanders in rather dopily. Everyone freezes.*

STEVE. Forgot me bag, didn't I? *[He notices that they are all staring at him]* So? *[Pause]* Alright, alright, don't want to disturb anything. I know when I'm not wanted. You can't win 'em all. I'm on me way! *[To* RICKIE*] Arrivederci! [Exit. They all stare after him, then turn to look at each other. There is a sudden release of tension]*

SAMMIE. Steve!

ELAINE. You got it!

RICKIE [*now it is she who is outraged*]. Hey, no, that's not what I meant at all! Hold on! That's out of the question! Steve is not available for this! Forget it!

SAMMIE. No, he's ideal. Really! You want someone who's reliable. Dependable. Nice. Not too bright. That's Steve!

RICKIE. Now hold your horses! I can't believe I'm hearing this! That is my boyfriend that you're talking about! [*Pause*] And what do you mean by 'not too bright'?

ELAINE. Sammie's right, though. And look: you've never kissed him in public, have you?

RICKIE. No...

ELAINE. And we can trust him, can't we?

RICKIE. I suppose so.

SAMMIE. Well, we can't ask *Ronnie* to do it, can we?

LISA. Nobody's asked *me* yet! And the idea is revolting! What am *I* supposed to do? Run around being lovey-dovey with him? Let him touch me up? Gaze into his big blue eyes?

RICKIE. They're brown, actually.

LISA [*ignoring her*]. Hold his hand? Rest my head on

his manly bosom? My prince... My hero... *[Firmly]* I can't do it.

ELAINE *[equally firmly]*. But you have to. Do you *want* to be crucified? Do you *want* to be victim of the month in the gutter press?

SAMMIE *[persuasively]*. Come on. You've only got to act a bit. And you know Steve. He's a nice guy. He's harmless.

RICKIE *[indignant]*. Well thank you once again!!

SALLY. And where do *I* come into this?

RICKIE *[still angry]*. Fair enough – I did say that you had a key role to play. The answer, darling, is *Gus*. You've been burbling about Gus and his bloody *Chronicle* for days now. *[Stopping* SALLY*'s incipient objection with a gesture]* No, just think about it carefully. What other music correspondent could we get to come over here tonight, raring to go, willing to give the world *our* version of the story?

SALLY. Why should he come over here so quickly?

RICKIE. Because, sweetie, you've got something he wants!!

SALLY. Eh? What are you talking about?

RICKIE *[sings]* 'When a man loves a woman...' You

will be the bait to lure him over. *[SALLY is thunderstruck]* So what's wrong? I don't see any problem. You like him, don't you? He fancies you, doesn't he?

SALLY. Well, yes...

SAMMIE. Come on, he's been sniffing round your National Front for ages. At least that's what *you've* been telling us.

SALLY. Well, in point of fact...

RICKIE. Don't say it – you're still a virgin!

SALLY *[really outraged]*. No, of course not!

RICKIE. That's something at least!

SAMMIE. But with *Gus*...? No?

SALLY *looks unhappy, nods negatively.* SAMMIE *and* RICKIE *give each other meaningful looks.*

RICKIE. Oh, Jesus wept!

ELAINE. No, no, that's even better! If he hasn't got to first base yet, he'll be over like a flash when you ring him up in, er *[Looking at her watch]* five minutes' time?

SALLY. You're asking me to... *[With a great effort]*

prostitute myself!?

ELAINE. No, dear, just to do some acting. *[To* LISA, *forcefully]* Just as Lisa will be doing. *[To* RICKIE*]* And Steve. Rickie, you'll talk to him, won't you? *[*RICKIE *nods unhappily]* It's only for a few hours, perhaps for a day or so. Just to kill that photo. *[Giving* RICKIE *the phone]* Ring him. He must be at Lennie's by now – it's only round the corner. Tell him why we need him.

RICKIE *[getting up]*. I'll use the phone in the bedroom. I wish I'd kept my mouth shut! Steve is not going to like this, not one little bit! *[Exit]*

ELAINE *[to* LISA*]*. Lisa, you'll have to be careful in public for a while.

LISA. How can I ask Vero to put up with this charade?

ELAINE *[to* LISA*]*. What is she, dear?

SAMMIE. A bloody banker.

LISA. She's in international financial services. Based in London.

ELAINE *[to* LISA*]*. Well, she can explain to you better than anyone what you stand to lose financially if that photo hits the Press and we don't do anything about it. *[Offering the phone]* Ring her now. It's a separate line. No time to waste.

LISA. She's coming over tonight anyway.

ELAINE. Good, couldn't be better. *[To* SALLY*]* Then you ring Gus, *now*. You do know his number?

SAMMIE. It's written on her heart in golden letters.

SALLY. Oh, shut up.

ELAINE *[giving* SALLY *the phone]*. Here. Tell him to come over as quick as poss. He can listen to the new material. Take some photos. Let him scoop Lisa and Steve *being affectionate together.*

LISA. Ugh!

ELAINE. And make it convincing!

SALLY *[pointedly taking the phone as far away as possible to ring* GUS*]*. Hello. Yes, it's me. *[Long pause]* Sally! *[Dying of embarrassment]* You know! *[Pause. The other girls crane forward]* So you haven't forgotten me! *[Pause. Gasps of relief]* Oh, go on, you're embarrassing me! *[Pause. Elaine makes encouraging gestures]* Oh no. *[Pause. They crane forward again, concerned]* Oh yes. *[Pause. Relief]* Oh no. *[Pause.* SAMMIE *points to the phone, making kissing motions]* Well, perhaps. *[Pause. Gestures of exasperation, strangling, etc.]* No, surely not! *[Pause. Despair]* Oh, alright. As soon as you can. We'll play you the new songs. *[Pause. Relief again]* No, don't start that again! *[Pause.* ELAINE *waves her fist at*

SALLY] No. No. Oh, alright. *[Seductively]* But only if you're my Gussie-Wussie! *[Pause. The others look at each other in disbelief]* Alright. O.K. *Ciao.*

SAMMIE. Jesus, building the Panama Canal was less work! Who's this 'Gussie-Wussie', then?

SALLY. Piss off!

SAMMIE. O.K., why don't you just say: 'Hi mate, this is your big night, so why doncha pick up a packet of Extra Sensitive and get on over 'ere for a quickie?'?

ELAINE. Don't be so horrible, Sammie!

Nobody has noticed RICKIE *re-enter with* VERO. RICKIE *coughs.*

VERO. Sorry. I hope I'm not disturbing anything? Rickie here let me in.

RICKIE *[apologetically].* Actually I didn't need to. The front door was open. Steve always forgets to shut it properly. That's probably how the fans get in. *[To* ELAINE*]* Sorry, Elaine.

Pause. The general reaction to VERO *is cool. Even* LISA *holds back.*

ELAINE. Hello, Vero. *[To the girls]* Look, let's get this stuff cleared away and finish the washing up. You girls can help me. Lisa can entertain her guest. We'll be in the kitchen. *[Exeunt with the remains of the takeaway meal]*

[5]

VERO. That wasn't a terribly warm welcome, was it?

LISA. No. But don't take it seriously. Come here! *[They kiss]* Still, it's a difficult situation now. You know what will happen when that photo gets into the popular newspapers?

VERO. O.K. You're a youth band. Being gay is not part of the image, I know. But does it matter? It's a modern world out there. So: with this photo you come out – you know, out of the gay closet, right? Then everything's in the open. That would be respected, wouldn't it?

LISA. No, it doesn't work like that over here. People *pretend* to be tolerant, but, well...

VERO. They're hypocrites?

LISA. I don't like this either, but we have to play it by the rules. I never worried about it much before...

VERO. Worried about what?

LISA. D'ya know what the others say? We're a *clean* act, know what I mean? We have a bit of a giggle sometimes, but no drugs, no orgies, no kinky stuff. If we get into the headlines the wrong way, we lose the fans. That's what *they* reckon. Maybe they're right. Those kids are very young. *[Moving away]* Anyway, I've got something to tell you. And you won't like it.

VERO. We've got to split up, right? *[Angry]* Well, I'll tell you this. They can go screw themselves. I've only just found you. I love you. *[Softer]* You turn me on. *[Pause]* I'm going to fight this, Lisa. Aren't you going to help me?

LISA *[looking at her, then taking her hands]*. You're lovely. Really. *[Breaking away again]* No, it's not as bad as that. You know Steve?

VERO. The roadie? Rickie's boyfriend?

LISA. He looks after the sound equipment. Does that sort of thing. Well, he and I are going to pretend to be together, just for the Press. Then we can kill this other story. That's the plan.

VERO. It's pathetic.

LISA. It wasn't my idea.

VERO. It's still pathetic. I can't believe it. You're going to *do things* with this man in public, right? Like – *what*? How far do you have to go before the rest of the world thinks you're straight? Can you live with this, Lisa? And what do you actually have to *do*? Do tell me please.

LISA. Come on, just relax. It's only for show. Sally knows a music correspondent, Gus. He's a complete pillock. He's coming round tonight to do a profile of the band, with photos. You can stay – just keep out of the photographs. You say you love me. Prove it. Do it for me.

VERO. Whose idea was it then?

LISA. Elaine's.

VERO. Your manager? Oh. Actually, she's O.K.

LISA. She's not really our manager. She looks after us on tour. She's made a lot of money out of the band. *[With a gesture]* Just look at this enormous house! Ronnie de Silver, our agent, he really runs the money side. He's coming round tonight as well. You're going to like him!!

VERO. Was that your famous British irony? Is he some kind of M.C.P.?

LISA. M.C.P.?

VERO. Male chauvinist pig. You know? Superfluous human material for immediate disposal? Castration candidate? Useless piece of shit? In words of one syllable: a *man*.

LISA. Oh! Actually, male chauvinist pig fits Ronnie quite well, though you're probably putting it too mildly.

VERO [*suddenly angry*]. How come that a girl band needs some jerk of a man playing Mr. Important?

LISA [*ironical*]. Sometimes we little girls need to feel a strong male hand on our shoulder.

VERO [*angry*]. No you don't! [*Softer*] Not when I'm around you don't.

LISA. You're fantastic, Vero. [*As they embrace again,* SALLY *enters*]

SALLY [*hugely embarrassed*]. Oh, sorry. I didn't want to disturb anything... er...

VERO. Hey, you never saw two women kiss each other?

SALLY [*floundering*]. Oh, no, look, sorry...

VERO. Women screw each other too. Perhaps you didn't know that. [*Advancing on* SALLY] Would you like to know more about it?

SALLY [*fleeing in panic*]. I'll go and see if the others have finished. I think I heard Ronnie's voice. Er. Be right back. [*Exit*]

VERO. You just do that.

LISA *[laughing]*. Oh, Vero, that wasn't nice at all!

VERO. She looked at us like we both had two heads or something.

LISA. She's very young. But, seriously now, we're going to have to go easy for a while. In public, *and* in front of the girls. Some of them are not quite on our wavelength, are they? As we saw just now!

VERO. This Ronnie creep – what's his part in all this?

LISA. He's an old friend of Elaine's. He and Elaine have known each other a long time now.

VERO. They were together, were they?

LISA. Elaine was really spaced out. She was a fan of one of the groups that he used to manage back then, the Jesus Explosion, you know, except back then they were called Hotrod Hardy and the Stiffs. It was before they discovered beads and kaftans.

VERO. I can remember them. They were amazing. They had dozens of enormous security men to keep all the fans off.

LISA. Elaine was a groupie. But the Stiffs weren't good enough for her. She wanted Hotrod. One night after a concert in Leeds, she climbed into his dressing-room through a skylight – she was dead skinny in those days – and sort of *disrobed herself* in front of him.

VERO. And I can guess what happened!

LISA. No you can't. He almost had a heart-attack. Girls weren't his bag. Not at all! He loved his mum; he collected antique eggcups, and he had a thing going with one of the security men. It must have been a *very* stressful experience for him.

VERO. So, what *did* happen?

LISA. Ronnie appeared at the right moment, and kind of *peeled her off* Hotrod and took her back to his lair and... well... you know.

VERO. I like Elaine. I can't imagine her doing it with a guy like that.

LISA *[with disgust]*. I can. *[Pause.* VERO *looks at* LISA*]*

VERO. What do you mean?

LISA. Everybody makes a mistake sometime, don't they? Well, Ronnie was mine. *[Pause]* No, the earth didn't move with Ronnie! *He* didn't move very much either. It just sort of *happened. [Pause]* It didn't *do* anything for me at all. Nothing at all.

VERO *[quietly]*. You never told me about it.

LISA. You never asked me about men, did you? Only women.

VERO. Lisa, I can't be jealous of you with men. *[Pause]* But it makes me angry, though. *[Pause]* Hey, sing me something!

LISA. Really?

VERO. Yeah. But not the commercial stuff – the singles crap. Something from the new L.P. Sing me one of those ballads that *you* wrote.

LISA. Ah, I know the one you want to hear! The one I wrote just after we met. The one that *you* wrote.

VERO. I didn't write it, Lisa. Maybe I gave you some of the ideas, though. I told you that you had to choose, didn't I?

LISA. And I chose you.

VERO. No, I didn't mean that. I meant *[Pause]* you had to choose between what *you* wanted and what *they* wanted. Between who you are and who they want you to be. I still don't know what you chose. You're still pretending, aren't you?

LISA. I grew up in a small town where you *had* to pretend.

VERO. Like the Midwest, right?

LISA. Yes, something like that.

VERO. Well, you're in the big city now. *Be yourself.* Remember that first Christmas, when we pulled a Christmas cracker and out came a funny hat and a toy and a bit of paper with a motto on it? And the motto said: 'Be yourself.'

LISA *[laughing].* No it didn't! They're always jokes in crackers. What it said was: 'Be yourself – it's the only job that no-one in the world can do better than you can!'

VERO. I don't think that's silly at all... *[Pause]* But sing me the song.

LISA. O.K., but you've got to imagine the whole group, and music. Not just me on my own. Alright?

VERO. Alright.

[6]

[SONG 3: Listen to Your Heart]

LISA *sings.* ELAINE, RONNIE, RICKIE, SALLY *and* SAMMIE *have crept in and taken up position. The lighting changes, the backing music comes on and* RICKIE, SALLY *and* SAMMIE *join in the refrain.*

VERO. You know what, you girls are good!

RICKIE *[bowing]*. Thank you! Thank you! Want to hear the rest?

VERO. You should release it as a single!

RONNIE *[interrupting]*. Oh no, ladies, let's be realistic!

RICKIE. Oh, come on, Ronnie.

RONNIE. This song is *not* a commercial proposition. This is *not* what our teenies want! But there could be a market niche for a more *uptempo* version! If you know what I mean? Something for *adults*. Change the text around slightly. You've got to tell it like it is! *[Sings his version of* Listen to Your Heart, *theatrically, and with appropriately lascivious gestures]*

> There is something you should do
> There's someone who can always help you
> He may be older than your friends
> But he knows what's best for you
>
> So let him show you things his way
> Give up what you know is unreal
> There's someone great for you to lay
> You can love the man you feel
>
> Just listen to the boss
> He knows what's best for you

Take him to your bed
And he'll teach you to screw

ELAINE *[laughing]*. You bastard, Ronnie, that wasn't Lisa's text at all! And we could never record those sort of lyrics!

RONNIE. Just trying to be helpful, honeybun. *[He kisses and gooses her]* Hey, your arse is getting flabby. *[To the girls]* And we haven't had a chance to say hello properly, have we? How are you lovely creatures keeping? *[He kisses and fondles* SALLY. VERO *watches this and his following actions with increasing outrage]*

SALLY. Aow!

RONNIE. Nice – keeping in shape! *[He turns to* RICKIE*]*

RICKIE. No fingers, Ronnie, O.K.? *[He kisses her chastely on the cheek and turns to* SAMMIE*]*

SAMMIE. No fingers! Or I might just cut them off. Or something else even. *[He kisses her very tentatively, then turns to* LISA*]*

RONNIE. And Lisa! Our little problem girl. The voice is nice, but something tells me that my little chicklet is under the weather at the moment? Am I right? Too much action? Too much excitement?

50

ELAINE. Ronnie... just lay off the girl, please?

RONNIE *[finally turning to* VERO, *whom he has been carefully ignoring].* But who is this?

ELAINE. This is Veronica. *[Conspiratorially] You know.*

VERO. No, I don't think he does. We've never met before. *[To* RONNIE*]* I don't actually think we've had the pleasure...?

RONNIE. Oh, entirely mine.

VERO. Mr. da Silva, wasn't it? Portuguese? Or Brazilian, perhaps?

RONNIE. *De Silver*, darling. You know, 'de' like the aristocracy, 'Silver' like the money. It's intended to suggest a blend of the traditional upper classes on the one hand and the people with the readies *[Gesture]* on the other.

VERO. And where do you *really* come from?

RONNIE *[surprised].* Is that relevant?

VERO. No, but let me guess.

SALLY *[interrupting].* He went to a snob school. And his real name's *Jonquil.*

VERO. Really! Now *I* had you down for the East End. Hackney, perhaps, or the Isle of Dogs. Somewhere round there. Jonquil! How exotic! It's not really *you*, though, is it?

SAMMIE *[spitefully]*. That's why he changed it.

VERO. I don't understand.

RONNIE. Put it like this... with a name like Jonquil you've got three choices in life: either you're very queer; or you're very tough; or you can run very fast.

VERO. And which were you?

RONNIE. Actually, none of them, dear. As Sexy Sammie here *[Indicating* SAMMIE*]* suggested... I changed my name instead.

SAMMIE. Eff off!

RONNIE *[mock-confidentially to* VERO*]*. Sammie has a tiny little problem – she's not getting her breakfast cereal. No crispies in her life at the moment. No crunchies and munchies. No snap, crackle and pop.

VERO *[genuinely puzzled]*. I beg your pardon?

RONNIE. She's not getting a regular Donald.

VERO *[still puzzled]*. Sorry?

RONNIE. A Donald Duck. *[Seeing that she still doesn't understand]* Oh dear! She's not getting *shagged*, darling. Know what I mean? Screwed? The deed of darkness? The beast with two backs? Americans *do* do it, I suppose? *[Pause]* But for Sammie, a personalised rescue is at hand. *[He blows her a kiss]* She's at the top of my list! *[*SAMMIE *gives him a one-finger salute]*

RICKIE *[with heavy sarcasm]*. You're so charming, Ronnie.

RONNIE *[bowing]*. It's the company I keep.

ELAINE. While we're on the subject, don't you think, *at your age*, that it's rather tasteless...?

RONNIE. Funny you should say that. Because you know what *you* remind me of, Elaine?

ELAINE. No?

RONNIE. The British Museum.

ELAINE *[suspicious]*. How come?

RONNIE. It's got lots of interesting things to do and see, but everything's so *old*.

SAMMIE *[unnecessarily]*. Yeah, fossils and old bones.

SALLY. Ha, ha, look who's talking.

RONNIE. No, that's a different museum. What I'm trying to say is: everyone's already *been there*. *[Leeringly]* If you know what I mean by that. They don't charge admission. People just go in and out as they please.

ELAINE *[very angry]*. You bastard!

SALLY *[to* ELAINE, *meaning well]*. Don't listen to him. He's just a nasty old man.

SAMMIE. You can say that again!

SALLY *[to* RONNIE]. What about Rickie and me, then? What are we?

RONNIE *[to* VERO]. Rickie is a *nice girl*. She's the 'clever one'. Just in case, though, she prefers her boyfriends to be a bit on the thick side. And Sally...

SALLY *[challenging]*. What, then?

RONNIE *[still to* VERO]. I don't think Sally has much of a sex life these days. It used to be *oh so* different! Still, speaking as someone who has climbed that particular mountain, I can understand why nobody's queuing up for a piece of the action. Perhaps she's decided to save herself for Gus? Lucky fellow! *[The doorbell rings]* Ah, talk of the devil!

ELAINE. That will be Gus this time. Steve has got a key.

VERO *[to the girls]*. Jesus, how do you put up with this guy?

RICKIE. It's acting time, girls!

ELAINE. Everyone knows what they have to do! Ronnie, behave yourself. *Please*. Don't blow it.

RONNIE *[unconvincingly]*. I shall be the soul of discretion.

ELAINE. Vero, better if you kept out of the picture, sort of? *[Looking at her watch]* Where's Steve?

VERO *[still angry]*. Did you hear me: I said, how do you put up with this guy? *[But she moves to one side as* GUS *enters]*

RICKIE. Action stations!

[7]

GUS *[with exaggerated manner and giving himself a mimed fanfare]*. Da-dadada! She called. I came. I am here.

VERO *[aside]*. Oh god, this one's even worse!

GUS. Where is she, then? *[*SALLY *comes over to him]* This *[To the others about* SALLY*]* is one helluva girl. Hmmm! *[He chucks her under the chin like a horse-*

55

trader examining a horse]

SALLY. Hello, Gus.

GUS. The night is young! However – business before pleasure. *[To* RONNIE*]* Ronald, my man – too much!

RONNIE. You said it, baby, you said it.

VERO *[aside]*. I think I'm going to throw up.

GUS. I was summoned. *[He adjusts his shades]* And you said: action. Action is my trade. Tell!

ELAINE. We've got new material.

GUS *[uninterestedly]*. Oh, hello Elaine. *[To* RONNIE*]* So what kind of promotion were you thinking of? A pre-release package? I can't get a good camera team here tonight. *[Looking around sceptically]* And where are the musicians? You want to film it *here*?

ELAINE. No, we're still rehearsing the new material. We thought you might like a preview.

GUS. Of course. Action not words – that's my motto. *[To* RONNIE*]* But what's the sweat? Do we need to do this tonight? This lovely lady here *[He indicates* SALLY*]* and I have *pressing business*. No pun intended! *[He laughs at his own feeble joke]* That right, sweetheart?

RONNIE. We've got a scoop for you. Love has blossomed.

GUS. Oh wow!

RONNIE. We want it handled *sensitively*. We know you're the best. We need the *professional touch.*

VERO. I can't believe it!

GUS. Indeed, you chose well! You chose the right man! So – let's take it away! Speak on!

ELAINE. It's Lisa.

GUS. Lisa? That girl is cool. I can dig that. *[To* LISA*]* Hi, Lisa!

LISA *[with an effort]*. Hi, Gus.

GUS *[salaciously]*. Who's the dream-boy, then?

ELAINE. It's Steve.

GUS. Steve Angelo from Purple Orgasm? Hey! Way out, man!

RONNIE. No. No. Steve... erm... from the technical team here.

GUS. Oh. *[Losing interest]* Steve the roadie, right? She pregnant, then? God, aren't *any* of you chicks on the Pill? Well, it can be done, I suppose. Mood shots. An interview. I need some background. Where is he then?

RONNIE. He'll be here any moment! We thought, while we're waiting, the girls could run through one of the new songs?

GUS. Why not? Cool. Great. Let it swing, maestro!

[SONG 4: I Feel Alive Again]

[8]

Enter STEVE. LISA *rushes over to embrace him.*

LISA *[exaggeratedly kissing him]*. Oh, Steve, I've missed you so much!

STEVE *[taken aback]*. Er, what? *[*GUS *starts taking photos]*

GUS. Hey, too much! This is *heavy*!

LISA *[with faked passion]*. Oh, Steve...

GUS *[taking photos]*. Yeah! Great! This is *hot*! *[To* STEVE*]* Yeah, fantastic. Get her down on the chair! Go round behind her! Get her round the tits from behind! *[To* LISA*]* Smile! *[To* STEVE*]* Touch her bum!

STEVE *[floundering helplessly]*. Er, darling, I've missed you too.

GUS *[still taking photos]*. *[To* STEVE*]* Stand over her, you're her *man*! Give her your *physical presence*! *[To* LISA*]* Look up at him. Eat him with your eyes! *[To* SALLY*]* You're next, baby!

VERO *[catching* RICKIE*'s eye]*. This is sick.

RICKIE *[nodding]*. You're so right.

SALLY *[quietly to* RICKIE*]*. Do *I* have to go through with this, too?

RICKIE *[irritated]*. Until we're out of this you do everything short of having his baby, right?

GUS *[orgasmically, still taking photos]*. Yes! Yes! Oh, yes! Make it *physical*, man!

RONNIE *[to* SAMMIE, *suggestively]*. Just watching this makes me horny! Know what I mean?

SAMMIE. You're an animal.

RONNIE. Why don't we two go off somewhere to *relax* for a couple of minutes?

SAMMIE. A couple of minutes! What a lover boy! But aren't you overestimating your ability by about, er, ninety seconds?

RONNIE. You cheeky girl! But that's how I like 'em!

GUS *[to* ELAINE*]*. Aren't they cute?

ELAINE *[to* GUS*]*. Our love-birds! Young love! *[*LISA *winces]*

GUS *[to* ELAINE*]*. The photos will be great, but I need an interview. *[To* LISA *and* STEVE*]* Our readers will want to know *everything*. Like: Where did you meet? Did *you* fancy *him* first? *[Leering]* Or did *he* pull *you*? Where did you... *do it*, you know, the first time? Make it sound really romantic – they don't want it to be just a shag, that's *their* miserable lives, they want to read something different! You know, you're *showbiz*. When you're together, what do you drink? We need brand-names, for the plugs. We've got a couple of good deals set up, we just need to point the kids towards the right product! *[Leering again]* We know what he gives *you*, darling! But what have you bought *him*? We can feature that too, try and set up a contract afterwards for a long-term campaign. We could be talking big bucks!

The doorbell rings. Everyone freezes.

ELAINE *[to* SAMMIE*]*. Well, go and answer it! It'll be another bloody fan. *[*SAMMIE *exits. Everyone stares after her. Pause. She returns, leading* ALLAN*]*

SAMMIE. This is Allan. Not a fan, I'm afraid.

ALLAN. Hello. I've come about the photograph I took this afternoon.

RONNIE *[looking at* ELAINE*]*. Photograph?

ELAINE *[looking at* RONNIE*]*. Photograph!?

ALLAN. Yes, *photograph. [Everyone looks at someone else, thunderstruck:* RONNIE *and* ELAINE *look at each other, as do* LISA *and* VERO, RICKIE *and* SAMMIE, *and* SALLY *and* STEVE; GUS *lowers his camera and looks puzzled]*

GUS *[piqued]*. Hey, I thought *I* was taking the photos!

<u>End of the first part of the play</u>

PART TWO

[9]

LISA, RICKIE, SAMMIE *and* SALLY *sing.* ELAINE, RONNIE *and* GUS *watch and listen.* VERO *and* ALLAN *stand, separately, somewhat apart from the others.*

[SONG 5: We've Got the Music]

During the song, ELAINE *very pointedly signals to* SAMMIE, *who leaves the rest of the band, quickly goes over to* ALLAN *and lures him offstage. As they finish,* VERO *and* RICKIE *slip away together, as do* STEVE *and* LISA. SALLY *drifts across to* RONNIE, ELAINE *and* GUS.

ELAINE *[to* GUS*]*. Now wasn't that great?

RONNIE. Are we aiming at the nursery school market? *[He gets a black look from* ELAINE*]*

ELAINE *[to* GUS*]*. You can ignore Ronnie, he was born tone-deaf.

GUS. Well...

ELAINE *[to* GUS*]*. We wanted someone who *really* knows the scene – who *really* understands music – to have a preview. Someone like yourself, who knows how to write, who can put it across.

GUS. Though I say it myself – and in all modesty – you did well! Among those in the know, I am known as *the man who knows*! When they want style, they call for Gus! A fluent pen in the hands of a fluent mind! What I am saying is, like, What I *say*, *is*. My column is *where it is at*, and when I say that this *is* where music is at, that *is* where it is, man. Or where it's gonna be tomorrow. Do you read me?

RONNIE. No.

ELAINE *[to* GUS*].* No, what he means is: he always borrows *my* copy of the *Chronicle*. *[Kicking* RONNIE*]* Don't you, Ronnie?

RONNIE. Oh, yes.

GUS. Cool! Then I'll profile *this* song. *[To* RONNIE*]* Yeah, of course it draws strongly on a folk-influenced compositional tradition, but that tells us where this band comes from, doesn't it? It's a pastiche of Purple Orgasm, Toytown Massacre, maybe even early Jesus Explosion...

RONNIE *[interrupting salaciously].* That's Elaine's favourite band!

GUS. ...which obliterates conventional harmonic structures, that's obvious. Don't give me any of that post-structuralist crap, this song is at the *cutting-edge* of contemporary taste! It'll blow their minds! *[Portentously]* Let the music world take note. I have *said* it. I shall also *write* it. And it will *happen*.

RONNIE. Well, if people *do* want this sort of shit...

GUS *[irritated, to* ELAINE*]*. I don't think that Ronnie's heart is completely in this project?

ELAINE *[kicking* RONNIE *once again]*. Ronnie is just a tiny bit *tired*. Aren't you, darling? Too many nights out, too many girls! Who was it yesterday, dear? Sammie, perhaps? You haven't had *her* yet, have you?

GUS *[jokingly]*. You dirty dog! Well, as long as it wasn't Sally!

RONNIE [with mock innocence]. Oh, no!!

GUS. With so much good-looking tottie around, it must go to your head!

RONNIE. Ah, well... *[He catches* ELAINE'*s eye and stops abruptly]*

GUS *[to* ELAINE*]*. And why did you send one of the girls away? More dark secrets?

ELAINE *[exchanging glances with* RONNIE. *Then, to* GUS*]*. Sammie, you mean? Sammie's looking after our other guest. *[To* RONNIE, *with another kick]* Isn't she, darling?

RONNIE. Oh, yes, young Allan. *That's* his name!

ELAINE. He's doing a feature on this house for his magazine.

RONNIE. Is he?

ELAINE [giving RONNIE a black look]. Yes, you know, 'Top People, Top Houses' or something like that. Pretty boring stuff! Boring magazine! He's boring, too! But he won't be disturbing us, I promise you!

RONNIE. No, you won't be seeing him again this evening, I hope [Correcting himself quickly]... er, I expect.

ELAINE [to SALLY]. Sally, sweetheart, be a good girl and look after Gus for a moment? I'll go and sort out things in the kitchen. Ronnie, darling, why don't you go and watch the telly or something? [RONNIE and ELAINE exeunt]

[10]

GUS. Well, what are we going to do then? Why don't you and me go and take a look at your stamp collection? [Leering] I like the big, colourful ones. And I bet you've got some most interesting perforations!

SALLY. I don't know why you have to be so crude all the time.

66

GUS. I take it that it's my earthy sense of humour and healthy masculine directness that you can't tune into?

SALLY. No, I just think you talk an awful lot of rot. You don't have to put it on for *my* benefit, you know.

GUS. What you call rot, darling, may seem like, well, rot to *you*, but it comes straight from the powerhouse of modern music journalism.

SALLY. Well I just wish you'd give it a break and be more natural.

GUS *[closing in on her]*. Be more *natural*, eh? That sounds good to me!

SALLY. Why do you have to talk so primitive when other people are around?

GUS *[grabbing hold of her]*. If you prefer I can keep it for when we're alone. Like now!

SALLY. Hey!

GUS. There's no-one around. Nobody's going to walk in. What say we, er, hit the hay?

SALLY. No!

GUS *[jokingly]*. The carpet's nice and soft?

SALLY. I'm not that sort of girl!

GUS. I don't understand you. I work with lots of girls in the music business – Marty... Gina... Randy – and none of them are like this! *[Pause]* There's someone else, isn't there?

SALLY *[terribly shocked]*. You've done it with all those girls?

GUS *[off-balance]*. No. I didn't mean that. I just meant, sort of –

SALLY. I thought you liked me!

GUS. For godssake! For the last ten minutes I've been trying to *show* you how much I like you!

SALLY. No you haven't. You just wanted to do it on the carpet with me.

GUS. That was only a joke. *[Combatively]* Anyway, what's wrong with doing it on the carpet?

SALLY. That's the sort of thing that *Ronnie* does.

GUS *[jealously]*. What makes you say that? Don't tell me... you and Ronnie have...?

SALLY. I refuse to comment on that! And I don't think you're nice even to suggest it!

GUS. It was only a joke! Really! Can't you take a joke?

SALLY. I'm sick and tired of being treated like that! Everyone thinks I'm an easy lay. Well, I'm not an easy lay! I wish I'd never met you! You're not a gentleman! So there! *[Exit]*

GUS *[calling after her]*. And I thought you were a nice girl! With *Ronnie* of all people! How could you? That's awful! That's absolutely awful! *[To himself]* That guy is evil, man! Abusing these young girls like that. He needs to be sorted out. He needs to be punched. Sally, how could you do it with that creep? When you could have *me*? What sort of girl are you? *[Exit. Lighting change]*

[SONG 6: Some Girls (Go Dee Dee Dee)]

[11]

Spotlight on STEVE *and* LISA.

LISA. Acting is not your strongest suit, is it?

STEVE. Well, it was a very unnatural situation, wasn't it? *[Justifying himself]* Anyway, I had the feeling that you weren't enjoying it... with a *man*, like.

LISA. What's more important, you weren't enjoying it either, my dear, were you? You're not exactly Casanova! *[He is obviously deeply crestfallen]* Oh, dear, I didn't mean to be hurtful! Men are so touchy about that – I've never understood why.

STEVE. It doesn't work so well with Rickie and me.

LISA. Come on, now! You're kissing each other all the time. People even make jokes about it.

STEVE. Yeah, well... that's more for *public* consumption, isn't it? You know, when we're alone... it doesn't really work.

LISA. Well well well, who would've thought? *[Pause]* O.K. Let's be practical now. *What* doesn't work? Give me a demonstration!

STEVE *[horrified]*. Oh, no, I couldn't do that!

LISA. Come on, I'm a woman of the world! I've had sex with men before – though I'd prefer to forget most of them... I just want you to show me how you would normally, er, *go about it*, so to speak. *[He is appalled]* No, just kissing and things like that!

STEVE *[relieved]*. Thank heavens for that! I thought you meant...

LISA *[laughing]*. No, no! *[Then seriously]* But actually, there would be nothing wrong with that. You know, a sort of... therapy? And Vero wouldn't really be jealous. Not if it were a man. I don't *think* so. *[Seeing his reaction and laughing again]* No, come on, you're not in danger!

STEVE *[embarrassed]*. I don't think I can do it,

70

though. Cos I know you so well and cos of Rickie. *[Pause]* Look, can't you, sort of, give me a few tips, like? *[Squirming with embarrassment]* You know... the way to do it *properly*? Seduction, I mean.

LISA. I'm not the world's greatest expert on 'how men do it', properly or otherwise. But what we could do, since you seem rather shy *[He flinches]*, is reverse the roles: I'll play the man and you play the woman! I can show you the kind of things that men have tried on with me over the years.

STEVE. I don't think it would work.

LISA. Why not?

STEVE. Well, women are always passive, aren't they, so how could you play a man?

LISA *[giving him a sharp look]*. Steve, Steve, Steve. That was a *very* revealing statement! No wonder you've got problems! Vero and I may not have willies to wave around, but we *do* know how to give each other pleasure. *Actively*.

STEVE. So – which of you *is* the active one?

LISA *[with a sigh]*. I was waiting for that question. Steve, when two people love each other, they're *both* active. And it's *not* a question of who goes on top.

STEVE. Oh.

LISA. Let's see if we can act it out. You're, um, *Stephanie [He giggles]*, and I'm... er...*Lysander*!

STEVE. So *you're* going to seduce *me*? *[The lights dim]*

[12]

The lights go up to reveal SAMMIE *and* ALLAN *sitting cross-legged on the floor.*

SAMMIE. Lisa and Steve have been a couple *secretly* for a long time now. It's a very deep and affectionate relationship.

ALLAN. Well, naturally.

SAMMIE. You seldom come across two people who match each other *so well*.

ALLAN. Actually...

SAMMIE *[interrupting him]*. I can tell you *so much* about the happy couple. I don't know where to begin! We could start with Lisa's schooldays. Or Lisa at nursery school. She was always the life and soul of the party. A bundle of laughs.

ALLAN. Look...

SAMMIE *[interrupting him again]*. There's this wonderful story about Lisa and her guinea-pig when she was about six. Your readers will love it.

ALLAN *[exasperated]*. Hey, stop! Look, I really only wanted to talk to someone for a second about my photo. Remember? My photo? But ever since you let me in people have been talking about whatsernames and I haven't been able to get a word in edgeways.

SAMMIE *[seductively]*. Oh, you don't want to talk about your boring old photo, do you? You're in a house with four of the most lusted-after women in Britain. You're *alone* with one of them, for godssake. *[She puts her hand on his knee – to his great surprise]*

SALLY *enters.*

SALLY *[to* ALLAN*]*. Hello.

ALLAN. Hello.

SALLY *[to* SAMMIE*]*. I'm not disturbing anything, am I? *[She turns away from* SAMMIE *without waiting for an answer and gives* ALLAN *a big beaming smile]*

SAMMIE. You are actually.

SALLY *sits down between them.*

SALLY *[to* ALLAN*]*. We haven't really had an opportunity to talk yet, have we?

ALLAN. No, we haven't.

SALLY *[to* ALLAN, *affectedly]*. Because you seemed such a nice, gentlemanly person. Men with good manners are a dying breed – as I have recently had occasion to notice.

SAMMIE *[raising her eyes heavenwards]*. Oh god help us.

SALLY *[to* ALLAN*]*. The name was Allan, wasn't it?

ALLAN. That's right.

SALLY *[to* ALLAN, *sugary]*. *Allan*. What a nice name.

SAMMIE *[to* ALLAN*]*. Allan, there's something you really ought to know (if you haven't already noticed, of course): I suspect that there's a rather feeble seduction routine going on here.

ALLAN. Sorry?

SALLY *[to* SAMMIE*]*. When I walked in just now I assumed that that was what *you* were doing.

SAMMIE *[to* SALLY*]*. Don't push your luck, kid.

SALLY *[to* ALLAN*]*. I must apologise for my friend here. She's a little short on the social graces, but she means well.

SAMMIE *[to* SALLY*]*. Oh, really? *[To* ALLAN*]* I realise that you haven't had much opportunity yet to study the mating habits of the indigenous female population around here –

SALLY *[to* SAMMIE*]*. Sod off, you cow!

ALLAN. Um. Well...

SAMMIE *[to* ALLAN*]*. – but perhaps I can fill in a few of the details. The classic routine starts off well enough, with smooth opening gambits, but then it loses a lot of its class.

SALLY *[to* SAMMIE*]*. Why don't you just piss off?

SAMMIE *[to* ALLAN*]*. Perhaps I can demonstrate how it's done. We'll leave out the intellectual chit-chat and get on to the practical stuff. *[Adopting the same pose as* SALLY*]* So, you're down on the carpet, right, everything is nice and cosy, and you're sitting directly opposite dream boy. You cross your legs and you let your dress ride up a bit...

ALLAN *[naïvely]*. And?

SAMMIE *[matter-of-factly]*. Well it does work better if you're not wearing any knickers.

ALLAN. Oh! *[And he looks – too late – as* SALLY *quickly adjusts her position]*

SAMMIE. We ladies have been doing it for a long time now, haven't we? Couple of million years probably. *[To* SALLY*]* Am I right?

SALLY *[to* SAMMIE*]*. You're just a jealous bitch!

SAMMIE *[to* SALLY*]*. Jealous of what? Of *you*?

SALLY *[to* SAMMIE*]*. Yeah, of me!

SAMMIE *[to* SALLY*]*. Don't make me laugh!

SALLY *[to* SAMMIE*]*. Cos you can't get a man! They're frightened you might bite them!

ALLAN *[weakly]*. Er, ladies...

SAMMIE *[to* SALLY*]*. I'll bite *you* if you're not careful!

SALLY *[to* SAMMIE*]*. You and whose army?!

SAMMIE *[to* SALLY*]*. You cheeky bag!

SAMMIE *grabs angrily at* SALLY.

SALLY *[to* SAMMIE*]*. Hey, what are you doing?

SAMMIE *[to* SALLY*]*. I'll teach you a lesson!

ALLAN *[weakly]*. Er, look...

SALLY *[to* SAMMIE*]*. Let go of my tit!!

SAMMIE *[to* SALLY*]*. Give over, it's only padding! *[*SALLY *wallops her]* Aow, that hurt! *[And she wallops* SALLY *back]*

ALLAN *[weakly]*. Look, I do think...

SAMMIE *and* **SALLY** *[to* ALLAN, *almost simultaneously]*. You keep out of this!

SAMMIE *[to* ALLAN, *with ruffled dignity]*. I'm sorry, I got rather carried away.

SALLY *[snivelling and feeling her wounds gingerly as she gets up]*. I bet I got a bruise! It'll show up on TV! *[Waving her fist as she exits]* I'll get you for this!

SAMMIE *[shouting and following* SALLY*]*. Why don't you go and tell teacher then? I'll give you something that'll *really* show up! *[Lighting change]*

[SONG 7: Bunch of Fives]

[13]

Spotlight on VERO *and* RICKIE.

VERO. It's disgusting. There are four of you – five of you, with Elaine – and what happens? You let that creep of an agent tell you what to do, and you dance around trying to impress a man who hasn't got the intelligence of an *ant*. And now this stupid reporter has got you all over a barrel.

RICKIE *[not really listening].* I still think it was a good idea, but I don't like Steve having to pretend like that.

VERO. Who knows? He may even be enjoying it. You never know with men.

RICKIE. No! I can't believe that.

VERO. Grow up, Rickie, it wouldn't be the first time. Men are always looking for the next challenge, aren't they? They don't love with their whole body, the way women commit themselves. That's why it's so fantastic when two women love each other.

RICKIE. No offense, but I don't think it's natural. It's not the way nature wanted it to be.

VERO. So you're telling me it's no good when Lisa and I make love? That's crap. How do you know what it's like? You've never tried it.

RICKIE. I've never tried cannibalism either.

VERO. But you *do* know what it's like with *men*, don't you? And don't tell me you've never wanted to try something different! Come on, Rickie, be honest. Men are all over you, like they've got a trainer with a stopwatch right behind them. They're sweaty, they're usually half-drunk. They fumble around with your body. They push and shove. It's all a big performance. Trying to score points. They're not tender like women. *[Pause]* Could you imagine doing it with *me*? *[She takes hold of* RICKIE's *hands]*

RICKIE *[tremendously tense]*. No.

VERO. I could show you so much. Men don't know how to touch women. Only another woman really knows how to do that. Hmm! *[She lets go of* RICKIE's *hands]* Men don't understand women's bodies. They never have done. Did you know that they discovered *America* before they found the clitoris!

RICKIE. I know. We did that at university. In the first year. We had this really trendy lecturer...

VERO *[genuinely surprised]*. You went to college? Of course, you're the 'clever one', aren't you?

RICKIE *walks away from* VERO *and then turns and looks at her thoughtfully. She is offended. Pause.*

RICKIE. Did *you* know that the two blokes – the one who discovered the clitoris and the one who discovered America – had the same name?

VERO. Sorry, I don't get it.

RICKIE. The anatomist was a guy called Mateo Colon. He was Italian too.

VERO. Yes... ? Sorry, I'm still not with you.

RICKIE *[taking her revenge].* Did *you* go to college?

VERO. Yeah, of course I did.

RICKIE. And they never told you about someone called Cristóbal Colón? You know? The guy who discovered America?

VERO. Now I get you. That was his Spanish name, wasn't it?

RICKIE *[ironical].* Hey! Well done!

VERO. O.K., O.K. I'm sorry. I didn't mean to be rude.

RICKIE. Then tell me this: why *shouldn't* a girl from a pop group have an education? I got my B.A. I worked for it, too.

VERO. Rickie, stop. This is going all the wrong way. I'm not a snob. Really.

RICKIE. Do you patronise Lisa like this?

VERO. No, of course not. I respect her very much.

RICKIE. Then respect me too. And accept that I'm different to you. I like *men*. I love them, sometimes. Even silly ones like Steve, bless him. He's lousy in bed. We haven't got very far yet. But when I want him to touch me like that, I'll show him how to do it. I don't need an expert. I don't need an Olympic champion. I want someone like *him*.

VERO. That's all I want, too. And some respect.

RICKIE *[singing]*. 'Don't you want somebody to love?'

VERO. Oh, I know that song!

RICKIE *[singing]*. 'Don't you need somebody to love?'

VERO. But it's so hard for us sometimes. It's not illegal, what we do, but the way people look at us... You can't imagine it, Rickie.

RICKIE. No, I really can't. I don't know *what* you do, Vero. I don't know *why* you do it. And I don't even know *how* you do it. But if you and Lisa need to do things like that, then it's O.K. with me. *[Pause]* But let me ask you something, Vero. Do you trust Lisa?

VERO. Of course.

RICKIE. But you don't trust Steve.

VERO. No. Do you?

RICKIE. Steve's a very quiet guy. I've known Lisa longer than you have...

VERO. But not the way *I* know her!

RICKIE. They're supposed to be playing the loving couple, kissing and touching each other. Do you really think they'll leave it at that? Anyway, I reckon that Lisa's more likely to try something on with him than Steve is with her.

VERO. Well, there's only one way to find out. Let's go and see what they're doing!

RICKIE. Alright! *[Exeunt together]*

[14]

Spotlight on RONNIE *and* ELAINE.

ELAINE. *There* you are! I've been looking for you everywhere!

RONNIE *[peevishly]*. You didn't have to keep shutting me up like that!

ELAINE. Nobody has ever succeeded in shutting *you* up for very long, Ronnie, but it was important that Gus didn't get too close to that reporter. Not until after he's done his story on our lovebirds.

RONNIE. Gus is too stupid to notice anything! He's not exactly the full shilling, is he? Anyway, what was all that about the house?

ELAINE. The reporter guy was showing a lot of interest in it. Maybe he's kinky about houses? Gus might have heard him. Anyway, he's in safe hands now. Sammie will have some fun with him, maybe keep him over the weekend, then we'll throw him out. By then Gus will have filed his story, perhaps even sold it to the dailies.

RONNIE. She won't sleep with him!

ELAINE. Why not? She hasn't had a boyfriend for a long time now. *[Looking at him intently]* Or do you mean: you don't *want* Sammie to sleep with him?

RONNIE *[playing cool]*. No skin off my nose if she does. But she won't.

ELAINE. You think she fancies *you*, don't you? *[Pause]* Ronnie, for them you're just a dirty old man. *[Silencing him, as he tries to say something]* No, let me finish. Lisa made a mistake. But only once. And when Sally needed her dad, or just an older man to cuddle, you took advantage of her. But you'll never get Rickie into bed.

RONNIE. I don't fancy Rickie.

ELAINE. No, she's too bright – and that's *why* you don't fancy her. And Sammie won't sleep with you either.

RONNIE. I don't see it that way. She's a challenge. I

like challenges. She's so frustrated, she's going to explode soon. O.K. So she's rude to me? There's tension in the air! But I'm going to break her. She's going to be on her knees, begging me for it.

ELAINE. But you don't *love* her, do you? *[Pause. Then, sentimentally]* Ronnie, what we had was quite good.

RONNIE. Yeah, but it's ancient history.

ELAINE. So are we, Ronnie. We're not young anymore.

RONNIE. You speak for yourself! And I'll have that girl on her back before you know it.

ELAINE. We'll see, won't we? Anyway, you've got a problem. Gus has got it into his head that you're after Sally –

RONNIE. Sally!?

ELAINE. Don't ask me where he got that idea from. But he's looking for you. He's foaming at the mouth. He's going to punch you out.

RONNIE. What?!

ELAINE. Well, I've done the best I can to help you. I told him you're queer.

84

RONNIE. You must be joking!

ELAINE. I said that your, er, crude routine with women was just a front, a cover, for your real passion for young men!

RONNIE. Well, thank you very much!

ELAINE. So when Gus appears, give him the heavy come-on, and do it *fast* – if you want to stay alive! O.K.?

Fade to black. Exeunt.

[15]

The lights come up to reveal ALLAN *talking to* LINDA *and* SHARON, *who are now disguised as workmen and carrying toolboxes, etc.*

ALLAN. I'm not sure that I'm allowed to just let you in like that. I'm mean, I don't live here. I'm only a visitor myself. What was it you said you wanted?

LINDA. We've come to read the meters, haven't we, sir!

ALLAN. Well, yes. Any particular sort?

LINDA. What do you mean?

ALLAN. Well, there are gas meters, and electricity meters. Some people have water meters, too... There are probably other sorts of meters as well!

LINDA. Yes, we need to look at all of 'em!

ALLAN. *Who* did you say you worked for?

LINDA. Oh, we work for the Authority! We come round here on a regular basis.

ALLAN. And why are there *two* of you? Seems rather unnecessary to me...

LINDA. Er... it's called work-spreading. You know, get two people to do the work of one. You must have heard about it? New government scheme! Very clever! It's a way of reducing the unemployment figures. Gets the kids off the streets. He's my apprentice.

SHARON. Yeah, I'm his apprentice.

ALLAN [*to* SHARON, *with a nod in the direction of* LINDA]. *You* are *his* apprentice? He's much too young! There's something very fishy going on here!

SHARON [*to* LINDA, *ready to give up the charade*]. Oh, come on, this is shitty...

ALLAN. *What* did you say?!

LINDA. No, no, um, that's the name of the scheme: Systematic Help in Training the Young. S-H-I-double T-Y. Spells 'shitty'. *Not* a pretty abbreviation, I'll grant you that, sir! But we *do* do our best.

ALLAN *[not completely convinced]*. Well, I suppose it's alright, then. Where would you like to start? In the cellar?

LINDA. No, we'll go upstairs first.

ALLAN. Upstairs? What sort of meters do they have upstairs?

SHARON. All kinds, mate. You'd be surprised.

ALLAN. Now I find that *very* hard to believe. And I am something of an expert on houses, you know. I mean, in a house like this, granted that it goes back to Queen Anne at least, though it has been renovated quite recently as you can see from the...

LINDA. Don't you worry your head about it, sir, let it be *our* concern! Take my word for it, we'll find what we're looking for!

SHARON. Oh yes! *[Exeunt]*

ALLAN. What strange young men. I hope they know what they're doing! *[Enter* SALLY*]* Hello again!

SALLY *[breezily]*. You must excuse my *ever* so

dramatic departure. Sammie gets *so* violent sometimes. It's good on stage, but she's got no self-control.

ALLAN. You didn't get hurt, I hope?

SALLY. Oh good heavens no! It wasn't as bad as it looked.

ALLAN *[indecisively]*. Well that's good then.

SALLY. But there *is* something that I'm upset about... *[Pause. No response from* ALLAN *]* I think you might have got the wrong impression of me from Sammie. I'm really not that sort of girl at all.

ALLAN. What do you mean?

SALLY *[coyly]*. Oh, this is awfully embarrassing! Well, like, what she said about my *knickers*.

ALLAN. You mean, that you don't wear any?

SALLY *[indignant]*. Of course I wear them! *[Pause]* Well, usually anyway. *[Quickly]* But I don't play those sort of tricks like what she said! That's just common!

ALLAN. Actually, I think it's rather a nice idea...

SALLY. I can see you don't believe me. I'll prove it. *[She turns away, then lifts her miniskirt to flash her* *beknickered bottom at him]* See, knickers!

ALLAN. Well I never...

SALLY. What?

ALLAN. They're the same as mine. You know, the same design.

SALLY. They could be from that unisex store.

ALLAN. My mum always buys my underwear for me.

SALLY. I bet they're not the same make as mine. These were *very* expensive. *[Naughtily]* Come on, fair's fair. I showed you mine. Now it's *your* turn!

ALLAN *[out of his depth]*. That would be a bit naughty, wouldn't it? I mean, what if someone came in? They might get the wrong impression!

SALLY. Come on, just a quick peek! Don't be a cowardy custard!

ALLAN. Oh, alright then. *[He fumbles to undo his trousers. Enter* GUS*]*

SALLY *[not seeing* GUS, *and moving towards* ALLAN*]*. Come on, let's have a good look!

GUS *[horrified]*. Sally, what do you think you're doing?

SALLY [*innocently*]. Well I showed him mine and now he's showing me his! Just to prove that I wasn't trying to seduce him back then when he thought I didn't have any knickers on!

GUS [*turning away, totally shocked*]. I can't believe it! I can't believe that this poor child has been corrupted like this! Pretty-boys aren't enough for this child-abuser – he's got inside the mind of a young girl, too! But there is *no way* that the monster is going to get away with it! I came to this house in good faith! Let that be put on record! The *Chronicle* is not mocked! The worm will bite back! When the dailies get this story, it'll be like feeding time at the London Zoo! You are dead, Ronnie, dead! [*Exit*]

ALLAN. What's wrong with him?

SALLY [*puzzled*]. And what's *Ronnie* got to do with it?

Fade to black. Exeunt.

[16]

Spotlight on LISA *and* STEVE.

LISA. There are different ways of doing it, Steve. There are different types of *men*. For instance, there's the *physically pushy type*. They're very common. We're at a party, and they're playing a slow number, so: come on Stephanie! *[She grabs hold of* STEVE*]* He runs his hands up and down your shoulders and back, like this. There's no point, of course. You aren't going to fall over if he lets go, and you don't need a massage. It can't possibly turn him on. He's feeling the knobbly bits at the back of your bra. Or how sweaty you are. You're both rather smelly. You're thinking: this is pathetic! He's probably thinking that *you're* thinking, This guy is a sensualist, he must be a fantastic lover. And then it happens, bang! His hands slip down onto your bum, ever so natural like, as if you're not supposed to notice, but you feel his whole body tingling, he's thinking: *at last* he's got his hands on your dirty bits, and this is where the party really begins!! Then he starts fumbling.

STEVE *[breaking from her grip].* That's not the way I'd do it. And you're not taking it seriously!

LISA. Alright, too much cynical lesbian commentary, I know! Let's take another one, then. There's the *sexual mathematician*, for example. *[Laughing]* No, I won't touch you this time! This one's easy to explain. His attitude is that if you chat up enough women, one of them is bound to cooperate. All you need to do is find the magic number 'n'. It could be a hundred and twenty! Think of chatting up a hundred and twenty women just to get *one* of them into bed!

STEVE. That's very cold-blooded. I'm not like that.

LISA. Well, good for you! Then there's the *cocktail*

mixer, who tries to get the girl drunk...

STEVE. That wouldn't work for me. I get drunk too quickly myself.

LISA. That was how Ronnie got *me* into bed.

STEVE *[rather shocked]*. Oh.

LISA. D'you want to hear how he seduced Sally?

STEVE *[shocked but fascinated]*. I don't think we should, should we?

LISA. Come on, Steve, we're all adults, and you might learn something useful. O.K., our next type is: the *bloodsucker*. It went like this. Sally's parents had just separated. She's an only child. She felt very lonely. She needed love. Uncle Ronnie was there to give it to her! *[Beckoning to* STEVE, *then clutching him in a passionate-looking embrace]* Come here! You poor little sweetheart!

STEVE. Eh?

LISA. Oh, for godssake try and act a bit! Put yourself in Sally's position! Men should do that more often anyway. How frightened and lonely she must have felt! He's giving the poor disturbed girl tenderness, but he hasn't got any emotion himself, he's sucking it out of *her*, and only *pretending* to help her. And all the while he's fingering her and opening up her

92

clothes... *[Exaggeratedly]* My little pet!

VERO *and* RICKIE *have entered unobserved, and watch the charade with mounting horror.*

STEVE *[now getting the hang of it]*. Oh, darling. Hold me tight!

LISA. Let me ease your hurt! *[Touching him sexually or manipulating his clothes]* Let me feel your pain!

STEVE *[beginning to enjoy the game]*. I need you!

LISA. You need someone in your life, someone who really cares. I can be that someone! Ah, your body feels so good!

STEVE. I feel so safe with you!

LISA. My darling!

VERO. This can't be happening! Lisa! How could you be so cruel? I trusted you, Lisa, really I did! And *this* is the reward!

LISA *[completely surprised]*. Oh, Vero, come on, it's not what you think!

VERO. No, but it's what I see and it's what I hear! If *that [Gesturing contemptuously at* STEVE*]* is what you want, then be my guest! *[Exit]*

LISA *[distraught]*. No, wait, I can explain! *[Exit]*

RICKIE *[tearful]*. How could you, Steve? I simply can't believe it. I thought you loved me. I thought you were a decent guy. How could you do this to me? *[She rushes out in the other direction]*

STEVE. Oh, dear... *[Pause] Oh, hell! [Exit. Lighting change for the song]*

[SONG 8: Don't Make a Fool of My Heart]

[17]

Spotlight on SAMMIE *and* ALLAN.

SAMMIE. Sorry I left you on your own like that. Sally ran into the garden and gave me the slip. But when I came back, you weren't there any more. *[Thoughtfully]* What have you been up to? You didn't see Sally by any chance?

ALLAN *[ingenuously]*. Oh, no.

SAMMIE. I'll let you into a secret. You're not supposed to talk to Gus. He's doing a story on the band, and they don't want anyone to spoil it, you know, with silly photos or anything. Oops! Me and my big mouth. I shouldn't have said that, but I don't like lying.

ALLAN. No, nor do I. Actually, I did see Sally again.

94

She's gone to have a lie-down. She's feeling upset. And I bumped into Gus, too.

SAMMIE. Really? Did he say anything?

ALLAN. Er, no. Well, he sort of shouted, and waved his arms about like a windmill, and then he rushed off. *[Pause]* Is life around here always so dramatic?

SAMMIE. You're *not* a reporter, are you?

ALLAN *[surprised]*. Did I say I was?

SAMMIE. You've had half of Britain's most famous girl group offering themselves to you on a plate.

ALLAN *[modestly]*. Oh, no.

SAMMIE. I've met a lot of reporters in the last couple of years. They usually make me want to wash my hands afterwards. Every male journalist I've ever met would have been in there like a ferret up a coal-scuttle. So what *are* you then? You're not a reporter. You wouldn't last two minutes on an average British newspaper.

ALLAN. No.

SAMMIE. But you did take a photo of Lisa and Vero.

ALLAN. Yes, I suppose so.

SAMMIE. And you're not a blackmailer, I'm sure of that.

ALLAN. Oh, no!

SAMMIE. So what *are* you then? *[Fade to black. Exeunt]*

[18]

The lights come up to reveal RONNIE, LINDA *and* SHARON. *The two 'workmen' are clutching their toolboxes and some items of flimsy underwear.*

RONNIE. I don't see why you should be looking for meters in the girls' bedrooms!

SHARON. Just doing our job, mate.

RONNIE. But the meters are all in the *cellar*. You must know that sort of thing, surely?

LINDA. Er. We were checking for leaks, sir. Purely routine, no cause for alarm!

RONNIE. And why are you carrying these... er... *[Taking them]* items of ladies' underwear?

LINDA. Well, when we check for leaks we have to clear the floor first.

SHARON *[importantly]*. It's all part of the job. It's all in the day's work.

RONNIE. But you must have been collecting these from different rooms. I mean *[Sorting them. He fails to notice the arrival of* GUS*]* this is Elaine's... and this is probably Rickie's... and this rather sexy one here could be Lisa's...

LINDA *[excitedly]*. That's Lisa's is it?

SHARON *[ditto]*. Oh, that's *nice*!

GUS. Knicker fetishism! I knew it – so this is where Sally learnt her tricks! Ronnie, you and I must talk! Now!

RONNIE *[in total panic]*. Oh, hello Gus, I can explain everything! I think? Oh, dear!

GUS *[indicating* LINDA *and* SHARON*]*. And who are *they*? Is this some clandestine meeting of sodomites or fetishists?

RONNIE *[realising what he has to do]*. Ah! Now funny you should say that... *[Exaggeratedly]* These good-looking hunks –

LINDA *[nonplussed]*. Eh?

SHARON *[getting worried]*. Now look, mate –

RONNIE [to LINDA and SHARON]. *What* did you say your names were?

LINDA. We didn't.

RONNIE [to GUS]. Ah, these casual pickups! [Campily] How embarrassing!

GUS. Ronnie, we have got to talk – man to man!

RONNIE. Man to man! What a thrilling thought! Gus, I've always felt that you and I could... *go places* together, you know, *do things*.

GUS [to LINDA and SHARON]. Has he been abusing you? Are you call-boys or something? [To SHARON] What's your name?

SHARON [ridiculously trying to deepen her voice]. It's Brad. My name's Brad.

LINDA. And I'm Jeff.

RONNIE. How could I ever forget! *Brad*. What a butch name! It always make me think of body-builders. [Tweaking at SHARON's biceps] But *you* haven't been to the gym recently, have you?

SHARON. Hey, stop touching me up!

RONNIE [to GUS]. Actually, I think I go more for Jeff. He's got a cute bum, hasn't he?

LINDA. Don't you touch *me*!

GUS *[flabbergasted]*. I am lost for words, man, lost for words.

RONNIE *[to* GUS*]*. Ah, I can see you're jealous! We can share them if you like. It'll be like a party on a submarine! *[Leering at* LINDA *grotesquely]* Hello, sailor!

LINDA. I've had enough of this!

RONNIE *[To* GUS*]*. And I'll give you first pick at the cherry-bowl. Of course, speaking for myself, I've always preferred the slim, girlish type...like this one here! *[Indicating* LINDA*]*

LINDA *[revealing her disguise]*. Look, you idiot, of course I'm girlish. What do you expect? – I *am* a girl!

SHARON *[also revealing her disguise]*. And I'm a girl too!

RONNIE. Oh. Oh dear.

GUS *[outraged]*. Transvestism as well! This is Sodom and Gomorrah! It's worse than New York! Ronnie, you are *sick*.

LINDA. Yeah, I second that. And I'm getting out of here!

SHARON. You're weird!

LINDA. You haven't got your chairs at home – any of you! *[Exeunt]*

GUS. Man, you are a serious case for therapy! I've never met anyone with so many perversions. No wonder that Sally is so mixed up. I better find that girl. Rescue her from this den of iniquity. *[Exit]*

RONNIE *[with a gasp of relief]*. Elaine, you've saved my life! *[Pause]* But I'm still going to kill you for this! *[Exit]*

[19]

Spotlight on SAMMIE *and* ALLAN.

SAMMIE. You're a student?

ALLAN. Yes.

SAMMIE. A *student*?!

ALLAN *[warming to his subject]*.[3] Yes, of graphic design. I've got architecture as a minor subject. I mean I don't mind graphic design and actually it's quite interesting but really I prefer architecture. I was

---

[3] This speech of Allan's can be shortened – or extended! – as required.

thinking of doing it the other way round, taking architecture as my major subject. Course back when I started I had the opportunity to do both subjects by opting for joint honours but at the time it did seem that it might be too strenuous cos they're both subjects with an important component of practical studies (and I bet you didn't know that about architecture but you have to do an awful lot of technical drawing and stuff like that) but if I do want to change my major subject now I need to do a fantastic term paper cos it's quite difficult to get into architecture as a major cos everyone thinks they can earn a lot of money later if they're an architect and that's why they make it so difficult for you to switch majors after your first year if you see what I mean?

SAMMIE *[politely]* That's really fascinating – but why were you taking photos of Lisa and Vero?

ALLAN. I wasn't.

SAMMIE. Yes you were.

ALLAN. I took a photo of the house.

SAMMIE. But Lisa and Vero were kissing.

ALLAN. Yes, it made quite a nice detail. But it wasn't important.

SAMMIE. *It wasn't important*? There has been total panic under this roof because of that photo!

ALLAN. Yes, it's a nice roof. They don't build them like that anymore.

SAMMIE. What in hell's name were you doing taking photos of this stupid house?

ALLAN. That's typical! I've just told you, but you don't listen! Nobody in this house seems to listen to *anyone*. You're all too busy boasting and showing off and trying to seduce people. I need the photo for my term paper. I want to do *architecture* as my major subject, remember? And it's not a 'stupid house' at all – even if it's full of stupid people – it's one of the most beautiful houses in the country. God knows how you lot came to own it, though.

SAMMIE. Oh.

ALLAN. 'Oh' indeed!

SAMMIE *[recovering her balance]*. But you do realise why everyone was so worried about the photo?

ALLAN. Well, I do *now*. *[Pause]* Sammie, when I rang your bell I just wanted to ask, sort of, could I use the photo? Some people don't like you taking photos of their houses. Then I got dragged in here. It's like a madhouse. Isn't *anyone* in the music business normal?

SAMMIE. The girls are alright, actually. Even Sally, though she gets on my tit sometimes. She's just young. Lisa's very sweet and kind, and Rickie's a very sensible sort of person. I'm a bit of a horror, I suppose!

ALLAN *[spontaneously]*. No, you're not – you're really nice.

SAMMIE *[surprised]*. Well, thank you!

ALLAN *[quickly changing the subject]*. But the blokes are awful. That Ronnie, for example – and the other guy, Gus, the rock journalist. Are they for real?

Enter GUS, *looking distraught.*

SAMMIE *[spotting* GUS *before* ALLAN *does, and putting a warning finger to her lips]*. Shhhh!

GUS. That Ronnie is sick! Seriously disturbed!

SAMMIE. Oh, hello Gus. *[To* ALLAN*]* You haven't really met Gus yet, have you? Actually I was told to keep you away from him. For reasons that don't matter any more. *[To* GUS*]* This is Allan, he's interested in *architecture*.

GUS *[rudely ignoring* ALLAN*]*. The man is an abomination! He shouldn't be unleashed on innocent young girls!

SAMMIE *[looking around in an exaggerated manner]*. Innocent young girls? Where? Which way did *they* go?

GUS. Putting their tender little bodies and delicate young minds in the groping hands of that degenerate! That pervert!

SAMMIE. We're talking about Ronnie, I suppose? Yawn, yawn... He *is* a dirty old man. A groper. But a *pervert*?

GUS. He does it with knickers... and transvestites... and group sex... and young boys!

SAMMIE. *Ronnie*? He hasn't got the imagination. His idea of heaven is a *Playboy* centrefold with ten per cent more silicone.

GUS. But I saw him doing perverted things!

SAMMIE. I'm sure you didn't. Ronnie is the most boringly heterosexual man you'll ever meet. The only relationships he has with women are gymnastic ones. Except perhaps Elaine...

GUS. But it was Elaine who told me that he was queer!

SAMMIE *[tremendously amused]*. Ronnie *queer*? Oh dear, you *have* been conned!

GUS. I've been tricked – and Sally is in mortal peril! He lusts after her!

SAMMIE. Ronnie and *Sally*? *[To* ALLAN*]* Well, I

suppose there *was* this thing between them a few years back...

GUS. I knew it! She is trapped! He has woven his gross spell over her poor little psyche. A man whose only aim – I quote! – is to *have his victims on the carpet*. A man without moral scruples of any kind – a trickster, a common salesman – battening like an old leech on the talents of these fine young women! The public must be warned at once! Pretending to be a pervert so that he can get at young girls! I'm going to punch him when I see him!

SAMMIE. Well, Gus, before you turn on the rough stuff, I think we ought to make sure that he really *is* after Sally. After all, as I said, Ronnie's not very choosy. Anything in a skirt will do.

GUS. That poor, helpless girl!

SAMMIE. I mean, he's tried to get into my knickers often enough. He even offered me a solo career if I, er, you know...

ALLAN. Well, that would be great, wouldn't it?

SAMMIE. Not at that price it wouldn't. Anyway, I can't sing solo. I just do the 'doo wah wahs' and 'hey babies' in the background on most of our recordings.

ALLAN *[gallantly]*. I don't believe that!

SAMMIE. But Ronnie knows it. Perhaps he thinks I'm vain about going solo, but I'm not.

GUS [who hasn't been listening to them]. Isn't anyone listening to me? That poor girl is in danger!

SAMMIE. Well, let's see then! Allan can go and fetch him. [To GUS] We'll go and have a coffee in the kitchen and then we'll listen in to what Ronnie says. Do a bit of snooping, O.K.?

GUS [already moving towards the kitchen]. I think I need something stronger than a coffee!

SAMMIE [whispering to ALLAN]. Get Ronnie talking about *girls* – he loves talking about sex! But don't let him mention any names! Gus's imagination will do the rest! It should be a laugh!

ALLAN [perturbed]. Does he really fancy you?

SAMMIE. Now don't say you're worried! You *are* sweet! [She gives him a quick peck on the cheek]

GUS [querulously from offstage]. Where do you keep the stronger stuff?

SAMMIE. I'm coming! [To ALLAN, with a wink] Here we go! [Exeunt. Lighting change for the song]

[SONG 9: Hold Me Now]

[20]

The lights come up. RONNIE *and* ALLAN *are centre-stage.* SAMMIE *and* GUS *are eavesdropping on them.*

RONNIE *[facetiously]*. Young Allan! How goes it then? Still worrying about those silly old photos? What did you say that it was, that of which you purport to be a student, if you'll pardon my grammar?

ALLAN. Graphic design. Well, with architecture as a minor subject.Although I was thinking of changing them round, you know, doing archictecture as my major...

RONNIE *[interrupting him with a grand gesture]*. What a waste of time for a red-blooded young man like yourself! What a waste! Books and buildings – how dead can you get?

ALLAN. Oh, I do admit that *you're* in a *much* more entertaining line of business, of course.

RONNIE. Indeed, you can say that again. Literally: the business of entertainment.

ALLAN. Working with fascinating people.

RONNIE. The job does have its moments.

ALLAN. Working with *really interesting* people.

RONNIE *[rising to the bait].* Aaah! What *you* mean is: working with sex-hungry young women! *[Winking]* Am I right?

SAMMIE. Is he talking about *us*?

ALLAN. No, I just thought it must be nice...

RONNIE *[warming to his subject].* Have you seen our girls when they *really* get going? Giving it all they've got! On stage for thousands! On TV, for millions! Everything up front! Hot! Steamy! Oh wow!

ALLAN. It must be wonderful, working so closely with such lovely girls. So intimately. I suppose you have your favourites?

RONNIE *[lewdly].* What do you mean by *have*?

SAMMIE *[to* GUS*].* Just listen to him! He's sick! And you know who he's talking about, don't you?

GUS. It had better not be Sally!

ALLAN. Well, I've noticed you looking at Sa... Oops! Now, now! Gentlemen never mention names! But you know who I mean.

RONNIE. Oh, indeed I do! *[Lyrically]* The way she runs her hand through her hair when she's reading or thinking about something. *[Mimes]* Like this. And again. And again. Her hair's fine, but she keeps on doing it. The little tart!

SAMMIE *[genuinely outraged]*. What a pig!

GUS *[angry]*. I'll have him for breakfast!

ALLAN. But it's a subconscious action when they do that, isn't it?

RONNIE. No, she's thinking about it!

ALLAN. What do you mean – *it*?

RONNIE. She's thinking about who could be looking at her. Fancying her. Her little heart is going pit-a-pat! She's thinking about *me*!

SAMMIE. Oh dear.

GUS *[getting angrier]*. I'll have him for lunch as well!

RONNIE. She's imagining *doing* it. With me!

ALLAN. Really?

RONNIE. She sees me as a father figure, you know.

SAMMIE. What!?

RONNIE. They all do. But then – all little girls fancy their daddy, don't they?

ALLAN. Oh, I don't know about that. We did this fantastic course called Foundations of Modern Society, and I can tell you that those old Freudian ideas are not held in much esteem these days. I think modern psychologists tend to believe...

RONNIE *[interrupting him]*. What can *you* possibly know about it, young Allan? What we're talking about here is the university of *life*. But I will tell you this. That girl is begging for it. Her nipples harden, her thighs tremble at the sight of me!

GUS *[even angrier]*. I'll make a dog's dinner of him!

SAMMIE *[grimly]*. I'll help.

GUS. As of now, he is *dead meat*!

RONNIE. She's got it under control. But only for the moment. She doesn't know what she's missing. And her little snatch is warming up! For *me*. Soon the dam will break! And when it happens, it'll be Gunfight at the O.K. Corral! It'll be the ultimate cosmic experience! It'll make the Fall of the Roman Empire look like a Sunday evening barbecue! It will be one god almighty comet-like explosion of libido, it'll...

GUS *[leaping out at him]*. No it won't! You bastard!

RONNIE. Hey! What? *[GUS hits him]* Aow! *[Holding his nose]* Oh, by dose!

Enter ELAINE, SALLY, LISA, VERO, STEVE *and* RICKIE, *who have all heard the noise that* RONNIE *is making. They,* SAMMIE *and* ALLAN *take up position around* GUS *and* RONNIE.

GUS [*to* RONNIE, *rubbing his hand, which obviously hurts*]. Look, O.K., no hard feelings, man. Alright? Violence is not my bag. But I can't let anyone take advantage of Sally here!

RONNIE. *Sally*?!

ELAINE [*running over to* RONNIE]. Oh, my poor darling, come to mummy!

RONNIE [*to* ELAINE, *plaintively*]. I didn't mean any harm! I don't understand what's going on. I think I'm too old for this lark...

SALLY [*to* GUS, *admiringly*]. Say that again, Gus! What you just said!

GUS [*to* SALLY]. I think there has been a quantum misunderstanding of my intentions.

RONNIE. *Your* intentions!

ELAINE [*comforting* RONNIE]. There, there.

SALLY [*to* GUS, *admiringly*]. You're fantastic!

LISA [*to* VERO]. That goes for us too, Vero. It was

harmless, really.

STEVE *[to* RICKIE*]*. Yes, truly it was. I'm so sorry, Rickie. It wasn't what it looked like.

LISA *[to* VERO*]*. We were just playacting, that's all.

VERO *[going over to* LISA*]*. O.K. I can see he's harmless. *[To* STEVE*]* And good for *his* sake that he *is*! *[To* LISA*]* It can work out, Lisa, but we have to be honest with each other. And we mustn't hide anything from the rest of the world. Why should we?

RICKIE *[holding out her arms to* STEVE*]*. Come here to me! There's nothing to forgive. And you're not harmless, darling. You know what? You're a tiger! *My* tiger!

ALLAN. I do still need to talk to someone about my photo of the house...

SAMMIE *[to* ALLAN*]*. Well, well. You seem to have worked some magic with that camera of yours. We can take some more photos if you like. I'll help you. I'll show you all the good angles!

ALLAN *[looking at the reconciled couples]*. Is this what they call a happy ending?

SAMMIE. Perhaps...

[SONG 10: Intimate Distance]

During the song, LISA *turns to look at* VERO, *who goes to stand beside her.*

LISA *[to* VERO*]*. And, anyway, it was only a kiss!

VERO *[laughing]*. And girls will be girls, won't they?

LISA. Yes, girls will be girls.

[SONG 11: Girls Will Be Girls]

<u>End of the play</u>